Saint Madeleine Sophie Barat

Foundress of the Society of the Sacred Heart

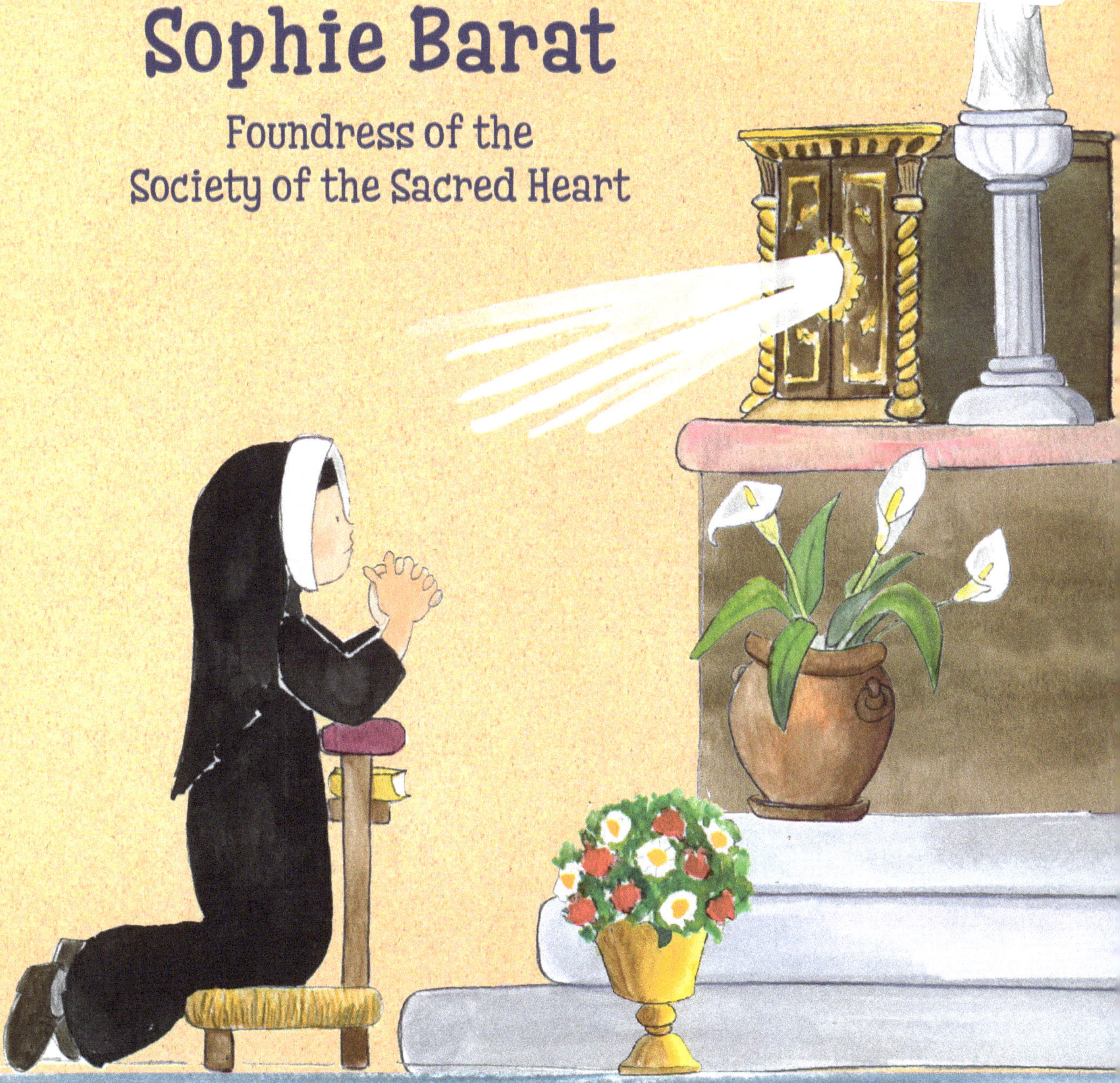

Marian Gabriel y Galán, RSCJ

Illustrations Pilar Campos • Translator Kim King, RSCJ

CONTENTS

I.	Joigny	5
II.	A Very Clever Girl	9
III.	Difficult Times	13
IV.	Paris	15
V.	Amiens: the First Sacred Heart School	19
VI.	We Will Call Her Mother Barat	21
VII.	A Lot of Work and a Lot of Travel	25
VIII.	The First Missionary	29
IX.	Joys and Difficulties	33
X.	Our Lord and the Children	37

CHAPTER I
Joigny

JOIGNY IS A SMALL TOWN in the Burgundy region of France. It is surrounded by beautiful vineyards. It has a big river with boats and with fishermen seated on the banks. The houses are simple; some are beautifully made with strong wooden beams that give them a dignified air. Sophie's house is smaller. It is one floor with two attics beneath the roof. In one of those areas, Sophie had her room. Like most of the houses in the village, her house also has a cellar to store the wine and a well for drawing water. Sophie's father was named Jacques Barat. He was a barrel-maker and spent his days working with wood. Her mother's name was Madeleine. She worked at home and was always busy.

And who is Sophie?

Sophie is a lively little girl who spends the day asking questions.

"Mother, people say that fire brought me into this world. Is that true?"

"Well, kind of, yes. You had not yet been born when a fire began in the village and came very close to the house. I was quite frightened and... then you were born."

"Was I frightened, too?"

"Yes, I think so. That's why you were born then. But you were so small that I did not think you would live."

Birth 12 December 1779

"Was I dying?"

"No, but you were so weak that they immediately took you to the church to be baptized. They gave you the name Madeleine Sophie and Louis, your brother, was your godfather, even though he was still fairly young."

"Oh! So that's why he demands so much and won't let me play in Father's vineyards as much as I would like to!"

"Yes, my daughter. That is true, but he is that way because Louis wants you to learn many things so that one day you become someone important."

"But I don't want to be someone important! I want to be like you. I really like helping around the house."

"God has a path for each of us. Who knows what God wants from you? He loves you very much."

"Of course! And surely God wants me to play more and study less because he loves me very much!"

CHAPTER II
A Very Clever Girl

AS HAS BEEN SAID, Sophie was very small, quite lively, and joyful. Everything interested her and she was forever asking questions. The parish priest from Saint Thibault, the church close to Sophie's home, sometimes seemed troubled when Sophie would perch upon a chair and ask questions he couldn't answer.

"She is a very clever girl," the priest had told her mother. "She is ready to make her first communion. I'd say that she has found favour with God. One day, she told me that giving one's heart to Jesus is the most joy one can give him, and that's why she wants to be all his. What do you think of that?"

Louis, the brother and godfather of Sophie, was preparing to be a priest.

He had left for the seminary, having already discovered that Sophie was very intelligent and that this gift of God was not to be wasted. But Louis was so extreme and demanding!

"Okay, Sophie. Today, you are going to learn one of Aesop's fables—in Latin, of course."

Bit by bit, Sophie's small table had been filling up with books: history, literature, mathematics, philosophy, including a book in Spanish, *Quixote!*

"Louis!" her mother said. "Let Sophie play with her friends! You have her shut into the attic with all of those thick books of yours."

The father, busy with his barrels, said nothing. But he did ask, "What is our son trying to make out of Sophie? After all, a girl becomes a woman, she gets married, she has children... this is the life that is her due."

Bit by bit, Sophie took a liking to her studies. Her clear intelligence developed, practically taking flight.

Sophie thought to herself, Louis is very severe, that's true. But he loves me and with him, I learn so many things!

CHAPTER III
Difficult Times

THE REVOLUTION WAS CAUSING many problems in France: Churches and convents were destroyed, priests were persecuted and put in prison. Louis had also been imprisoned.

"Eat, Mother! And stop crying—we are going to trust in God and you'll see that Louis will come out of prison."

Sophie had become quite a responsible young woman. She placed enormous trust in God. God was already the most important thing in her life. But she did not yet know what God wanted from her.

Mother and daughter prayed before the painting of the Sacred Heart that was in the kitchen. They asked that these difficult times would be over.

The Sacred Heart had heard them! What joy! Louis had been freed. He had not had an easy time of it. Louis was thin and serious... He didn't say anything, but he had plans for Sophie. Because he did not want his mother to suffer, he did not share these plans with her. He waited until the right moment.

One day he spoke with his sister.

"Listen, Sophie. I believe God has something in mind for you. We are going to go to Paris and you will continue your studies there. It is no longer possible to do so in Joigny."

"But Louis, what about our mother and father? We are going to leave them alone? What are you up to?"

As much as she tried, Sophie could not sway her brother. Should she obey him? Is that what God wanted for her? She asked for help so that her mother could accept this. Her father did not understand but kept on working and was silent about it.

Departure day had arrived. The spring sun was splendid. This year the river was flowing especially fast after the winter rains. The boat's horn sounded to begin the crossing. Sophie couldn't stop her tears.

"Why, God? Where are you taking me?"

Her mother embraced her tenderly and before she boarded the boat, she told Sophie, "Bundle up, my daughter!"

She couldn't say anything more because she was filled with emotion.

CHAPTER IV
Paris

1795
1799

WHAT HUSTLE AND BUSTLE in the streets! Sophie was stunned. How she missed the quiet and calm of Joigny. The trip had been long and tiring, but Sophie nonetheless felt great peace and security.

During the crossing, Sophie had been able to talk to God quite a bit and she dedicated herself to contemplating the clouds, the flocks of birds, the riverbanks, and the river itself that watered the green countryside. It began to seem to her that God was again saying, "Sophie, I want you to be completely mine."

This was all happening so quickly!

"Of course, this is Louis's way of doing things. If I can barely concentrate on my studies. I feel so very strange in this noisy city and now I miss my little corner of Joigny..."

"Listen Sophie, tomorrow you will have an interview with a priest who is a friend of mine. His name is Joseph Varin. He'd like to meet with you and ask some questions. I've spoken with him about you."

"But Louis, how could you not have talked with me first? You already know that this type of thing intimidates me. What does this Father Varin want from me? I've already told you that my wish is to be a Carmelite."

God entered more and more into the life of Sophie. It seemed that Sophie could do nothing but accept that which God wanted of her.

"I am glad to know you, Sophie. The revolution has been a disaster for the country and especially for the youth that are, after all, the future of France. It is important to educate the girls and the young and you have a formation that's rare for someone your age."

"I don't understand what you are proposing, Father. My wish is to be a Carmelite."

"Yes, yes... Louis has spoken with me about your desires to be a Carmelite, Sophie. But in the Carmel is not where God wants you. People are needed to educate the girls, to form them so that they in turn educate their children and the family. How does that seem to you, Sophie? Don't you believe that this is the path the Lord wants you to follow?"

Sophie said nothing. She did not yet see it clearly. Father Varin was talking about a kind of religious life that was different from the one she desired. Sophie trusted God. She had already learned the value of obedience.

This is how, on the morning of November 21, 1800, before a painting of the Virgin Mary, Sophie and three companions began a new life, promising to follow the Lord, no matter the cost.

Vows
21 November
1800

CHAPTER V
Amiens: the First Sacred Heart School

1801

AMIENS IS A BEAUTIFUL CITY. It has a river that reminded Sophie of Joigny. It is there that she and her companions began to teach a small group of girls. The house was tiny and poor. The girls were very happy because the religious were good and very caring toward them.

But... how tiring and how cold! From morning to night spent with the children! At least at night, when the students had gone to bed, the religious gathered by candlelight and spoke, joked, laughed, talked about how the day went, and spoke of God—which was what they liked the most.

"At last we are alone, Sisters!" Sophie said. "These little ones that God has put in our hands are quite content and they are learning many things."

"Yes, Sophie, but what little imps they can be with their comments and their desire to play all of the time!"

"This is true, but don't you feel joy when they listen to you? When they ask questions and want to know things?"

"Okay, okay... let's get going on peeling these potatoes and preparing the vegetables for tomorrow because in between classes, we do not have too much time."

"I'm hungry...!"

"Well, there's hardly anything in the pantry. See if there is something left over from the students' meal."

Sophie admired how the students discovered that Jesus loved them. Some had fared so poorly in the Revolution! And she also liked how they were learning the value of doing things well, their desire to learn, and how they were growing both on the outside and on the inside. This must be what it is to educate.

"You're a little bit idealistic, Sophie. If some of the students are badly behaved, we must punish them. But it seems as if you are an enemy of punishment."

"I think we would gain much more by being patient with them. I am convinced that it is only through love and goodness that we can attract them to the heart of Jesus."

So it was that among the laughter and the tiresome bits, the sisters busied themselves being sure the children learned and, at the same time, felt loved.

Throughout her whole life Sophie would remember these beginning times, in the first school that came to be in Amiens, which they like to call "the cradle" of the Society of the Sacred Heart.

CHAPTER VI
We Will Call Her Mother Barat

"DON'T YOU THINK SOPHIE is always too quiet?"

"Yes, of course. She is the youngest of us and somewhat shy. But I believe she is full of God on the inside."

"I see that she works a lot, though she is not hurried. And how the time flies when being around her! Can't you feel the peace she radiates?"

"It could be said that the joy that she has is because she lives only for the Lord and for the children."

Sophie was only twenty-three years old and already an excellent teacher. It seemed as if she had the gift of calling forth the best from her students.

One day...

"Come! Father Varin is here along with Louis Barat! What could they want?"

Father Varin gathered the sisters, saying that there was something important he wanted to tell them. Right from the start, he addressed Sophie and only afterward did he speak to everyone else.

"Sophie, do you want God's will above all else?"

"Of course. It is the only thing I want."

There was a question in Sophie's heart— *Why is he asking me this? Could it be that he doesn't know that my only desire is what God wants with my life?*

Now addressing everyone, Father Varin continued. "The moment has come for the community to have a superior. It is you all who must elect her. I ask that you now come before God and reflect on this."

But it didn't take much reflection—they all elected Sophie, who was speechless and almost trembling, not knowing what to say.

"Yes, Sophie, everyone wants it to be you. Don't turn away from this. I know already that you consider yourself too small. God is at work and makes great music with small instruments. Now you are this small instrument in his hands."

Sophie accepted.

"If you want this, my God, then I want it too. I shall be your small instrument."

The day had begun with rain, but a radiant sun was shining in the little community. They had someone who would direct the educational work they had in their hands.

One of the sisters said, "We have to find her a name..."

When the girls found out, they gave her the name without much thinking at all.

"We can call her Mother," said a bold and mischievous student.

"Yes!" they all said. "We will call her Mother Barat."

Everyone applauded and was happy.

"How lovely that sounds, 'Mother Barat'!"

CHAPTER VII
A Lot of Work and a Lot of Travel

SOPHIE, OR NOW, MOTHER BARAT, knew that there was a lot of work to be done. She did not feel capable and so she confided it all to the Heart of Jesus.

France passed through difficult times. The children and young people needed education. Mother Barat had many ideas. And she also had a dream: She saw many children and young people of all ages. Hundreds, thousands, of girls in need of educating. She dreamed of them on their knees before the Blessed Sacrament, exposed in a large monstrance with rays that extended to encompass the whole world.

Would that we could educate them all about the love of Jesus and in so doing, form a long chain of students who know how to bring the love of the Heart of Jesus to all parts of the world, and who know how to face difficulty with joy, courage, and a sense of duty...

She had to speak of this dream with the sisters. Soon, though, Mother Barat awoke from her dream. There was much work to be done.

"Mother Barat, some parents are here who want to enroll their daughters in the school. And others who want to propose founding a school in their city. They are influential people. The truth is, this is too much for us."

"Yes, yes... but it is also very important that we offer education to the children of the families most sorely in need."

Mother Barat reflected on the kind of education she wanted for the schools of the Sacred Heart. They needed to set up a Plan of Studies. Students needed to learn not only to be good Christians and to one day be good mothers to their families. To be able to change society, they needed a sound formation and needed to study much.

She shared her thinking about the style of education at Sacred Heart with the sisters. They listened attentively and also offered ideas themselves.

"To educate is not only about teaching lessons, however important this is. Above all, it is this: that each child open herself to truth, to love, to freedom... That she lives the experience of the love of Jesus. That she may discover the meaning of her life and work on behalf of others."

Sophie was now busy with new foundations and traveling a lot. And what travels they were! In horse drawn stagecoaches, on bumpy, muddy roadways, and with poor accommodations. How many hours and how many days, rolling along the roads of France.

"We're never going to get there!" complained the sisters who accompanied her.

"Don't you worry. We will arrive soon. Haven't you heard the saying that all boats arrive in port when it is God at the helm? So all stagecoaches arrive at their destination when God is guiding them."

Mother Barat had answers for everything.

"Yes, Mother, yes. But could you talk to your friend the coach driver about taking more care going over the bumps because otherwise, we are going to arrive all finely ground like flour! Don't you think there are too many trips?"

Whenever Mother Barat proposed something, if it was seen to be for the sake of educating more young people, it was done—whatever the price to pay.

CHAPTER VIII
The First Missionary

ONE DAY, MOTHER BARAT SAID, "Educating is like putting a seed in the ground and caring for it so that it grows and develops on its own. That strength is within every girl that we educate."

Another day, she said to the others, "A small seed can become a large tree. What do you say we plant a large tree in the garden?"

They replied, "Yes! Yes! We can plant a pine tree! Or, even better, a chestnut... or an oak... or an almond tree..."

"Ah, well... We will plant a cedar tree. A cedar is a very large tree that extends its branches toward the four directions, like the love of the Heart of Jesus that we want to bring to the whole world."

Over the years, the cedar grew and grew, just as the schools and houses of the Sacred Heart did. The reach of their branches went beyond the ocean and all the way to the New World.

It happened in this way:

Rose Philippine was an enthusiastic religious like none other. She dreamed of being a missionary and going to America. But she needed the permission of Mother Barat.

"Please, Mother Barat, allow me to go. I want to bring the love of the Heart of Jesus to faraway places, places beyond the ocean!"

"Let me think, Philippine. Going so far away, with so many dangers… We shall wait for a sign from God."

Waiting! This was very difficult for Philippine. But at last, Mother Barat allowed her to go along with four other sisters. It was an exciting moment.

"Goodbye! Goodbye to all of you! Take good care and write when you can."

The ship, the *Rebecca*, was sailing farther away from the coast of France and Mother Barat's eyes were filled with tears. *America is so far away. Perhaps they will not see each other again.* She remembered leaving her town of Joigny.

But in her heart, there was a new joy. *We already have the first missionaries of the Sacred Heart. Would that I could go too! But God wants me here in France.*

Months passed with no news of Philippine. At last, the first letter arrived and Mother Barat gathered the community to read it.

Life is hard here. And quite different from life in France. We live in a small house that could really be called a cabin. But we have the first students. We haven't got enough of anything except joy and trust in God. My companions are courageous, determined, and very good educators. As far as how I am… I am a bit of a mess. I do all that I can, without much success. I do not mind—God wants me small and poor. I dream of going to live among the Potawatomi. I do not know if that will ever come true.

Of course Philippine achieved her dream. Nothing would stand in her way. The Potawatomi gave her a name—"The Woman Who Prays Always." Philippine could not communicate with them because she did not know their language so she dedicated herself to prayer. It is said that when they learned of her death, they composed a beautiful poem in Philippine's honour.

CHAPTER IX
Joys and Difficulties

FRANCE ALREADY HAD MANY SCHOOLS of the Sacred Heart and had opened others in various countries. They all needed to be cared for. Thankfully, some students, caught up in the enthusiasm of Mother Barat and their teachers, dreamed of being Religious of the Sacred Heart themselves.

"We have to open a novitiate. God has blessed us with many vocations."

"How joyful these young novices are! And they sing like angels!"

Mother Barat opened the first novitiate of the Sacred Heart. When her work permitted it, she loved to be with the novices. Afterward, novitiates would be opened in other countries.

They had sent Pauline Perdrau, a young woman who wanted to be a novice, to the school at the Trinità dei Monti in Rome. She was an artist. For a long time, she had an image of the Virgin Mary in her mind.

"Reverend Mother, would you allow me to paint an image of the Virgin Mary on one of the walls of the cloister?"

The superior, having doubts but willing to see what came of it, permitted it. Pauline set to work. When her work was uncovered, there were many comments.

"Truth be told, the colours are quite garish. And besides that, a Virgin Mary in a hallway instead of in a church?"

"I for one don't dislike it. Actually, it inspires devotion in me and in the children. When they pass by, they love looking at her because she is a girl like themselves."

The Pope took an interest in the Virgin and had come to bless her. He liked the image very much. "We will call her Mater Admirabilis," he said.

But she is known around the world as "Mater," which is easier. And Mater became the image of the Virgin Mary present in all of the schools of the Sacred Heart.

If there were difficulties in America, there were also difficulties in France because of politics. After such efforts had been made, there were schools and convents that had to be closed. Mother Barat was sad, though she did not lose heart. She put all of her trust in God.

"What's wrong, Mother Barat? Are you sick?"

"No, I am not sick. But I am very sad. Some sisters that were so united before are no longer united. It seems as though they have forgotten the beginning times when spirits and hearts beat as one. They want to change the original Sacred Heart spirit. And I am asking myself whether I'll be the one to blame for it all."

Mother Barat prayed a lot. She wrote letters upon letters by lantern-light, with her quill pen and her inkwell, which was always full. She wanted to communicate with all of her daughters and share with them what she held in her heart. She was certain that one day they would all come back together and form one heart and one soul in the Heart of Jesus.

CHAPTER X
Our Lord and the Children

AFTER THE STORM CAME THE CALM. The Sacred Heart had heard Mother Barat and she had new-found energy and spirit for undertaking new foundations. But her health suffered for it. She even had to stay seated in a wicker wheelchair for months.

She did not travel as much now—letting other sisters do that. But her pen did not stop writing. She poured her counsel, her wishes, and most of all her care for each one, into her letters.

Mother Barat always said that what she liked most were Our Lord and the children. For that reason, insofar as she was able to, she surrounded herself with the children, especially the smallest ones, and would laugh at their goings-on, talk to them about Jesus, and have good times together. When a student was difficult, she would find a reason to bring her to the garden and listen to her attentively. What would she say so that these little ones would change and behave so well?

Just like her heart, the door to her room was always open to everyone: religious, students, families, those who were poor and needed help, and even a small cat who had just given birth slipped through her door to place her precious kittens at her feet.

By this time, Mother Barat was quite old. Bit by bit, her topic of conversation became always the same: the love of the Heart of Jesus. No one ever tired of listening to her, though. She lived in Paris now. She could still write letters and help out a bit, but more than anything, she dedicated herself to prayer.

She had discovered a quiet little corner of the chapel from which she could see the tabernacle. And she remained there, ever filled with prayer.

Those who observed her knew that the Heart of Jesus and the humble heart of Mother Barat exchanged their secrets and their love.

Death
25
May
1865

This story does not end here.

Though she died on May 25, 1865, Mother Barat continues to live in the heart of each student of the Sacred Heart, students whom she loves, and students for whom she prays.

Mother Barat is very generous in granting the graces that are asked of her.

Originally published in Madrid as *Santa Magdalena Sofía, Fundadora de la Sociedad del Sagrado Corazón*.

Copyright ©2020 Society of the Sacred Heart. All rights reserved. No part of this book may be reproduced in whole or in part, or stored in a retrieval system, or transmitted in any form or by any means, electronic, mechanical, photocopying, recording or otherwise, without written permission of the author.

ISBN: 978-0-9971329-8-4
Printed in the United States of America.

Illustrations: Pilar Campos
Book design: Peggy Nehmen, n-kcreative.com

Published by:

4120 Forest Park Avenue, St. Louis, MO 63108-2809 • 314-652-1500 • RSCJ.org

www.ingramcontent.com/pod-product-compliance
Lightning Source LLC
Chambersburg PA
CBHW061147010526
44118CB00026B/2899